Lucy English is a spoken word poet and novelist. She has toured widely in the UK and the US. With the South West Collective she co-wrote *Flash*, a multimedia spoken word show, which toured the UK in 2010–11, and also *Count Me In*, which toured from 2014–15. She ran a series of performances and workshops in Sri Lanka, India, Thailand and Taiwan for the British Council's Animating Literature Programme.

She is the co-organiser of the Mix Digital conferences at Bath Spa University and of Liberated Words, which curates, screens and creates poetry films.

Lucy English is a reader in creative writing at Bath Spa University. Her first collection of poetry, *Prayer to Imperfection*, was published by Burning Eye Books in 2015.

www.lucyenglish.com

@lucyenglish1

AF215111

The Book of Hours

Lucy English

Burning Eye

BurningEyeBooks
Never Knowingly
Mainstream

This edition published by Burning Eye Books 2018

www.burningeye.co.uk

@burningeyebooks

Burning Eye Books
15 West Hill, Portishead, BS20 6LG

ISBN 978-1-911570-37-0

The Book of Hours

CONTENTS

A MANUAL OF WONDER

Memories crash in my head. That night when we camped in
    the land
where great shadows of mountains rose above us
as we listened to the river churn.
How I sat with Rich in a room in the church
filled with stained glass and paintings of angels.
I had returned from a week of dark.

And next to that memory,
I was on the green hill in Radnor.
The storm clouds twisted through pastel over the river.
I said, 'I can do this. I can.'

Now I am silent. The light drains outside the cottage window.
My head is heavy. My back hurts. My brain is frozen.
I need to re-draw my days. Turn hours into new works of art.

I begin. I begin again. I make a new mark.
My brush touches canvas with blue. My pen slides across
    smooth paper.
A crow crosses the sky.
I draw this. The crow, black on the page before me.
I add touches of watercolour. Orange seeps into the blue.
    Then I write.

Begin with this. Begin here and do not stop.

LOOKING FOR EURFYL

We came here when you were
looking for Eurfyl, Uncle Glyn. He walked out in 1972
and never came back, you said.
Not your favourite uncle. A quiet man and thin.
He wore three ragged jumpers and ate dry crackers, you said.
What happened to him?

That warm day and the light so clear
it made the edges sharp on things,
like the great tit's song, *teacher, teacher*,
and the cluck of jackdaws. *Cluck.*
The A4 hummed a low note and a peacock squawked.
The gardens all fresh; late narcissi, wedding-white,
and the bright catalpa leaves nearly out.

January now and daffodils are pushing through.
a moss-filled pond and a sundial with no shadow.
Moss is the only green on trees. The cluck of jackdaws. *Cluck.*
Correct, correct, coming from the dismal yew.
You found his name on a certificate, you say.
Eurfyl Glyndwr. Died in 1988.
Died of a wasting disease in a Brighton flat.

The slop of the fountain in the pool.
The background slur of the London Road.

MR SKY

You were my neighbour all this winter, Mr Sky.
When I left my house you were trying to impress me
in your best shirt, all pink patterned with aubergine,
silks and satins with a new tie of rainbow.
On Sunday you wore gold trimmed with magenta.
You were the bold one, Mr Sky.

When it rained for seven days, even then you cheered me.
Your workaday suit was iridescent. A pigeon's breast
never shimmered like you did. Two-tone mauve and lavender
and grey like the softest wool socks.
Smoke in my fireplace and smoke in my eyes.
I opened my door for you, Mr Sky.

I loved you, but you were the mad one.
When I locked you out after a late binge
you threw the moss off the roof tiles.
You rattled the windows and kicked at the door latch.
I was afraid, so I slept in the cupboard. Wrapped in the cat's
    blanket.
I couldn't keep my drink, could I, Mr Sky?

But in the morning, I was sober and guilty.
When I opened the curtains there you were.
Your face pressed to the window. You, all pink fresh and sweet-
    smelling.
You, in your best gold and aubergine;
silk and satin with a new tie of sunrise.

LAVENDER BLUES

Lavender blue, Dilly, Dilly.
Lavender green.
You be a king, Dilly, Dilly.
I'll be your queen.

I'll be your queen, Dilly, Dilly.
You be my king.
Take your guitar, Dilly, Dilly,
and sing, Dilly, sing.

You'll never be angry
about signing on.
You'll never be angry
when the money has gone.

We wouldn't worry
about getting old.
And not paying the rent
and being homeless and cold.

You'd never be angry
about politicians or God,
and say no one listens
to us, they're all sods.

You'd be kind and generous
and smile at me and sing.
If I was your queen, Dilly, Dilly,
and you were a king.

I'll be your queen, Dilly, Dilly.
You be my king.
So take your guitar, Dilly, Dilly,
and sing the blues, Dilly, sing.

DO NOTHING

I will lie in bed and do nothing.
I was dreaming of lino floors and pastel blue cupboards.
A Formica tabletop speckled like sand.
Lakes and rivers in the lino. Rivers of mud.
My chair was a ship
with a red plastic seat.

If I turn I can open the curtains
with my toe.
I used to think clouds were like pillows.
And the turn of an EasyJet landing at Lulsgate.
There's a crack in the ceiling looks like a river.
The delta end is near the window.
I'm in a plane looking down at the estuary.

Merging in strands. My hair on the pillow.
I used to think clouds were like pillows.
I jump from the plane and I'm hurtling down.
I'm shocked. Clouds are just water. Droplets of mist.
I fall from the plane and onto my bed.
Soft. I am soft.

Under the covers.
I'm thinking of you. I'm not fifty-four.
I'm seventeen and my tummy's flat.
But it's not you. It's my first love.
I stroked his hand and he pulled my panties down.
We did it on the floor. In the car. Behind the shed.
In the garden. On the floor.
But seventeen means too much crying.

He was crying and I was crying.
So I'm not seventeen. I am seven.
The pillow is a snow slope I can jump on.
Tiny me in a snow field.
On a cloud. The sun's gone in.
I was dreaming of a kitchen. Was I?

A red plastic seat?
I'm fifty-four and it's my day off.
Get up. Breakfast. Coffee. Toast.

THE SHADOW

I said to Rich, 'I do not understand this country.
These freeways lined with motel signs.
These great empty sweeps of land and sky.
I feel so unimportant. So unconnected.

'In my cottage I used to walk beyond my garden
and straight into the woodland. That was my refuge,
my consolation. I stood there under the arms of oak and birch,
my feet sunk into the layers of leaves. And I was held, Rich,
I was held.'

I was crying then. He walked across the room and took my hand.
'Come with me,' he whispered. I trusted him and so I did.
We drove for four hours. Way beyond any town.
Way beyond the freeway and right into that landscape
that left me blank with wonder and arctic cold.

'Can't you feel it?' he said, and I said, 'I feel nothing.'
And he said, 'Look.' I looked. At the sky. The snow
on the distant mountain range. He said, 'No. At us.'

The shadow of our little car against the land
touched the winter grass but did not bend it.

'That's the only mark we should make on earth,' he said.

He wound the window down and the air blasted in.
The smell of nearly winter and the song of distant birds.

OUR LADY OF THE ROCKS

Dear Children, I beseech you to turn your hearts to love.
The burning love you find in the driest of places.
Grass still grows in the crack of a rock
and twisted roots push further into the sand.
The red sand ripples with the force of the wind.

Dear Children, I beseech you to go down the desert road,
where the thorn on the dry bush pierces your skin
and your blood is the colour of the crooked strata.
There are many layers between life and no life
and I am the purple flower that blooms without rain.

You are the dirt in the wind and the discarded blue plastic.
The branches stripped white and the flakes of old paper.
I am the wet split in the stone and the salt crust of the seashore.
The scorch of the sun on the pelt of the lizard.
The last circle of water on the bed of the lake.

Dear Children, I told you all which was necessary.
I gave you this knowledge which you must carry with dignity.
Think of me now and how I shed tears at this vision.
You must decide to surrender everything to me.
You must decide to surrender everything.

DARK PLACE

I used to wear a salmon dress,
green woollen tights, red shoes.
Blonde hair to my waist,
I danced with a poet at the rooftop party.

Now I live in a basement with black-out drapes.
The sunlight hurts me and I'm afraid of news.
There's a lost planet behind the moon
and when it moves it will impact on Earth.

The poet said I would like it here,
but he's not a poet, he never was.
He gives me milk to make me ill.
He gives me bread to make me bleed.

There's a devil shouting through the wall,
'Lock her up! Lock her up!'
I think I am already dead.
My salmon dress smells of fish,
my red shoes are grey with mould.

THE RETREAT

I have not blow-dried my hair for a week
or thought about which outfit I should wear,
or revamped my Facebook status or sent a Tweet,
or cooked a complicated meal.

I ate tinned fish and apples.
I read nine books and wrote nine poems.
I'm wearing musty jeans and an old T-shirt.
My hair has found its own fashion.

There is another life I didn't have
and I feel it like a silent twin beside me
who sits and looks out of the garden room window
at the rain clouds coming down from Crug Mawr.

THE LITANY OF THE SAINTS

Lord, have mercy on us.
Christ, have mercy on us.
Lord, have mercy on us.
God, the Father of Heaven, have mercy on us.
God the Son, Redeemer of the World, have mercy on us.
God the Holy Ghost, have mercy on us.
Holy Mother of God, pray for us.

St Anthony, the protector of animals, pray for our kindness.
St Ramon, the patron saint of emptiness, pray for our silence.
St Jerome, protector of abandoned children, pray for our
    tolerance.
St James, the pilgrim, let us come back safely from holidays.
St Stephen, the saint of bricklayers, help us to make wise
    decisions.
St Joseph of Cupertino, give us success in examinations.
St Valentine, the saint of love, protect us from fainting.
St David, the saint of poets, give us divine inspiration.

St Rita, saint of loneliness, pray for us to be bolder.
St Monica of alcoholics, pray for us to stay sober.
St Louise of social workers, give us good guidance.
Mary Magdalene, who knew about passion, pray for us to love
    wiser.

From a sudden and unprovided death, O Lord, deliver us.
From tailbacks and junction closures, O Lord, deliver us.
From lightning and tempest, O Lord, deliver us.
From supermarket queues and lack of small change, O Lord,
    deliver us.
From the scourge of earthquake, O Lord, deliver us.
From famine and war, O Lord, deliver us.
From work-based functions in conference rooms, O Lord,
    deliver us.
From eternal damnation, O Lord, deliver us.

STONE LIFE

White outside and white inside.
A brown sofa and a tin trunk to put my books on.
Flagstone floors are dark dark grey.
Tartan blankets the colours of the Marches' fields.
Slate green. Wood pigeon. Mole.

'What do you do all day?' you ask me.
I get up at six and light the fire.
Soot on my fingers, I make porridge.
Over breakfast I look at maps.
Where shall I walk today? I don't care about the rain.

Every time I walk I see a new thing.
Yesterday a bullfinch, today a cloud
settles on the far hill and wraps it.
Back inside the rain comes. It doesn't matter.
I read *Natural Planting* and *Wild Gardens*.

'Are you happy?' you ask me.
I'm not sure I know, but I am still.
There's a pub down the road but I don't go there.
When I walk past I can smell real cider,
such a sweet vinegary cloud. Hear high laughter.

'Are you happy?' you ask me.
I'm not sure I know, but I am still.
But in my dreams I am that crazy thing.
I laugh, tear off my clothes, run up the stairs.
You laugh, we fuck, we shout, we fuck.

I wake in a snap to silence.
White outside and white inside.
I get up at six and light the fire.

SATURDAY

Smells like stone floor and beeswaxed wood.
A whiff of damp
on a mouldy patch by the door
where the paint has peeled.

Smells like old newspapers
folded musty in the firebox.
Last night's wood ash and spent matches.
Split beech logs. Dried-up sap.

And coffee. Always coffee.
Tangy with an edge of bite.
Homemade marmalade and toast charcoal.
Red wine on the cork of the midnight bottle
and tomato stains of unwashed lasagne pans.

Smells like hair still smelling of beech smoke.
Smells like skin still smelling of bed.
Garlic, Merlot and sweaty dressing gown.
Wash it away with lavender shower gel.
But not now. Not right now. Not right now.

FROM THIS TRAIN

April comes crafty as an urban fox.
Steps through mud over the stones
by the iron jigsaw bridge.

He sits under a parkland bench
and thinks of fern-green dreams.
Nettle burrows and dandelion seeds.

But this story collapses.
I catch a sound in my hands.
The sparrow song. Sip sip sip.

A stone in a wall for a moment
looks like a crouching fox
with its tail wrapped round.

From this train the houses
now become fields dug up
and shredded, becoming more houses.

I fear nuclear power.
A concrete landscape and buried trees.
The president cuts the pink ribbon.

WEIRD WEATHER

Last April was so hot we swam in the river.
On the path was a puddle black with tadpoles.
Most were dead and smelled of rotting seaweed.
The others squirmed into the tyre tracks.

I wanted to walk to the river
and see anemones and wild garlic in the grass,
not a puddle with black things.
Did they know that they were dying?

I dreamt that the Ice Age was coming.
Snow fields reached to the edge of the city.
An avalanche was predicted.
We panicked and ran from our houses.

My daughter was a fish girl
with pink gills like feathered seaweed.
I wrapped her in cellophane and put her in my pocket.
But I couldn't carry water in my pocket.

My son was four years old and was with his father.
The phones were down so I couldn't reach them.
I hoped his dad had wrapped him in an army blanket.
I hoped his dad had listened to the warnings.

I dreamt I saw my son in the street.
He stood still in the running people.
I was relieved because he was grown up.
He was wearing an army coat.

The young man wore a grey coat
but his face was cold with sadness.
He said, 'Do they know they are dying?'

NOW IS THE TIME

Now is the time to leave.
Because I have seen the special places.

When I look out of the kitchen window
at the line of unmown grass above the wall.
The feathered grass, just in seed, and underneath
yellow vetch and purple knapweed.
The pond green of the hazel hedge.

I see the light on the canal water in Dorsoduro.
This was April, after a short burst of rain.
The city freshly washed. The puddles on the path
already faded. I wore a mint green dress
and cream leather sandals.

My weekend holdall. Cream leather. Light.
A station platform. November afternoon.
Across the rails the power station cooling towers
stream white into the falling sky.
Sunday, and the train is late.

And the duck pond by the Old Library.
Leaves on the water. The grey sky in the water.
Me, four years old in my red duffel coat.
I throw bread to the ducks,
but they will not come.

THE WOMAN AT THE WINDOW

How did I get to be this old? I saw myself in the shop front
    window
and I saw my grandma. With her baggy tweed coat,
her shopping bag of potatoes and that squint she had
when the sun was too bright.

Inside I am still young. I know this.
My hair is fine and my skin is soft. I know this.
I still jig when 'Dancing Queen' plays over the airwaves
and I laugh like a drain when Tom and Jerry fight on the stairs.

When we came here that April the cherry blossom
was out in Prospect Park and the old men smiled at us.
We bought fresh bagels, cream cheese and salmon,
from the bakery in Vanderbilt. We ate them in the street

and the cheese ran down my chin, and how you laughed at me!
That night by your window we saw the street lights come on.
You said they were switched on just for us.
In your room near the Bergen Street subway.

I am still young. I know this. Before, this concrete was woodland.
There are no high rises here but black oak and maples.
The grass grows to the edge where the grey mud meets
    seawater
and the Canada geese gather for their long flight north.

AT THE CHURCH OF ST ISSUI

'I give thee most humble and hearty thanks
for all thy goodness and loving kindness to me.
Especially for this… and this… and this.'

I saw two sheep.
One was shorn and lay across the path.
I thought he was dead, but when I stamped
he scrambled up and fatly ran

back to his mam, the shaggy one.
He knelt down and butted her to drink.
They were the same size,
but she was hot and cross.
Her fleece peeled in dirty strips.
She kicked him off. He would be lamb chops soon.

I saw the statue of the saint
in his chapel up the hill.
He was grey and made of lead.
There was a vase of dead tulips
and an empty box which said *This way up*.

On the way back I saw the well,
an oozy patch in a stony hole.
Brown water seeped through the gunk
and bled down the muddy slope.

On a scrappy bush were strands of hair
and red rags tied to make a wish.

This… and this… and this.

MAY QUEEN

Her knicker lace was cow parsley.
Her blouse was the froth of the May tree.
Her skirt was patched with red campions and stitchwort
and she was dancing down the lanes.

Wild girl, where are you now?
With your blue eyes and your careless laugh
and your apple-blossom skin
and your pissy smell
and the mud splashed up your thighs
and your hair all anyhow.

You're in the deep woods, stretched out
under the hazel and hornbeam.
The unfolding blanket of green
and the wet bed of bluebells.
The strange pale light over the bluebells.
And the song of a wren.
And the bluebells.

QUIET SOUNDS

The clouds hold in sound.
Hold it down. A wood pigeon croons
with the chuck of a pheasant.
Up the valley a sheep blahs.

Fine rain makes no noise, no drips,
and the stream over the pebbles, under the bridge,
is background dribble
to a high-up plane's faint shhh.

The kitchen clock marks time's neat click.
I sneeze three times. A letter?
Four. Something better? A cow complains.
A crow caws back.

Mmmmmm. Says the fridge
to the rumble of another plane.
My inner ear can now hear
the weight of hush.

OLD GREEN THINGS

Wednesdays are green. The sheen on a lilac leaf.
Those blousy flowers have dropped
and are scruffy seed heads.
But the leaf remains clean. Balanced one against the other,
tangled in panicles of white hydrangeas.
Such smooth green hearts. Still romantic.

Sun through the nettles. Their leaves translucent, jagged.
A whole plot of nettles. Butterfly food.
Nettle beer. Nettle gruel.
This ragged vegetable crop. In March better than spinach.
The only vegetable you grow, but the sun
doesn't bounce so gracefully off cabbage.

I am green. Ivy wrapped round a dead ash tree.
Slow-forming, not seeking out sunlight but witnessing it.
My leaves dusty. Turning inwards, I crawl up the wall
and inside to mangle bright things, like geraniums,
and block the windows.

A green stain on a bathtub.
Years and years and years and years of water dripping
the trace element of copper.
Green pipes corroded and the wet
mess soaked up by a shaggy bathmat.

I am sly. Insidious.
Old green thing.

A lilac tree when the bloom has gone.
An ivy plant creeping round the mossy pots.
A tired nettle bouncing off the sun.

THE NAMES OF TREES

Dear Rich,
In the park this evening there was low sun on blossom.
Prunus trees and whitebeam. Parkland trees.
Pink and white blossom against dark twigs
and pale leaves of ornamental chestnuts.
Clouds after rain, with a pinkish tinge.

A soft grey light. A man with a black and white dog.
A slice of sun at the base of the clouds.
I don't know why I walked back from work that way.
I usually go past the shops, but I was later tonight.
It wasn't dark and this is a safe place.

Dear Rich, I know you would laugh
at my suburban house in a tree-lined road.
My teaching job. A partner older than me.
With you it was as if each moment dazzled.
We were always moving, never settled.

That day I walked to your last place.
The Greyhound bus stopped near the store.
I walked past the car lot, and the factory block,
and down your street, a tree-lined street,
and the leaves were just out. Pale leaves,
and evening sun. Low light on bricks.
I didn't know the names of the trees.
It was your country. I didn't know the names of trees.

NIGHT WALK

It's half a mile from the pub to my B&B.
One turn off the road and into the lane.
Then the pub lights fade and I can't see my feet.
I forgot how dark it gets when there are no streetlights. And no
    moon.

And low clouds, and no torch, and I didn't bring my phone.
This is a Dark Sky Area. They are proud of that here.
This is dark. There are no stars.

I could go back, bleat for a lift, or light,
but I don't want to look like a stupid townie. So I step out,
my hands in front of me. Perhaps I can see shapes.
Yes. I can see the line of the hedge against the black.

Stop. Remember something about how long it takes for eyes to
    adjust.
Close my eyes. Count to twenty… sixty.

My other senses jolt.
I can smell the hedge. Greeny wet, and the grass, fresh, sweeter.
A small rustle. A field mouse? Shrew?

Open my eyes. It's not sight I have now but radar.
I can feel when I pass a gap in the hedge. The air is cooler
    through fingers.
And then a car roars down the lane. But it's not a car.
A huge tree. A loud tree above me!
Walking fast now and not scared. No. My pints of cider zapped.
I reach out hands and breathe right in… ahhhhhh.
Different smells. Mud, slush, rot, wet, sludge. A ditch and a
    drain…
and more roars as the wind up the lane…
and the trees are… shhhhhh.

Heart pumps. Boots clomp. Waterproofs crackle.
Stinks of plastic and cider fumes. I terrify rabbits and voles.

Even a fox will not cross me.
In the field the sheep have heard me, maaaa, maaaa.
In a far farm a dog roufs and again.
There's the pool of light from the windows.
I walk faster but don't want to go there.
Stay a monster in this night world.

Then something flaps past me. Big.
I almost scream but don't in awe. A barn owl.
Hunting ghost. Eerie white.
And feather silent.

DAISY CHAIN

Daisies on a lawn. White petals edged with pink.
Bright in the sun. Buttercups and dandelions in the field.
And daisies. Tough stalks and a ring of leaves.
On the lawn under the apple tree,
teenage girls doing backflips.

Bright eyes and messed-up hair. Bikini tops and tiny shorts.
Puppy limbs and pink skin. Then flopped
in the shade under apple blossom.
Making jewellery. A bracelet. A necklace.
A four-foot-long fragile daisy string.

Who made the first daisy chain? A mother and a Stone Age
    child?
They had no time with the scrape of flint on pigskin.
Or in the woods finding haws.
Footprints in the mud.
Daisies are not forest flowers.

Daisies grow in farmers' fields. Mown by sheep and cut with
    blades.
Two farmer's daughters. Not yet wed.
Stopped making cheese and bashing dough.
Flopped on the grass under the apple trees.
Picked a daisy. Split the stalk. Threaded it through.

Then another. A whispered secret.
Too soon shrivelled. Too soon spoiled.

THE RIVER GIRL

Here she comes, my June.
Rucksack on her back, she's home for the summer.
Dark hair across her shoulders.
She wears sandals and the long green dress I bought her.
She walks along the river path.

When she comes, my June,
I open the kitchen windows
and our house smells of fresh grass and marsh water.
Oh, she's full of stories! We're on the garden patio.
Watch the moths in the candlelight.

But at breakfast she's on her phone.
She's already making plans.
There's a thrush on the eaves. He's singing for his love.
He can't sing it loud enough. He sings each line over.
Then her phone rings again.

And she's off, my June. Off towards the river.
Rucksack on her back. Her boots on a string.
I say she must be careful, must be cautious.
But she walks by herself
through the salt marsh to the estuary.

When she's gone I wash the plates. Do the laundry.
Her dress is on the floor. Crumpled in a corner.
A thrush on the steps breaks open a snail.

SOLSTICE

Don't sleep.
It won't be dark until midnight.
We can walk through the dunes
to your friends on the beach.

The lanterns by the bonfire;
we can see the flicker from here.
The cold sand squeezes between our toes.
Start to run now, towards the sparks,
through the tough marram grass,
and you're shouting, 'Swim! Swim!'
You chuck off your shirt, and shorts,
leave a trail of clothes on the sand,
and I strip too, bra off, down to my pants,
tits bounce, I run after you, a pink streak.

The bonfire crew cheer us on.
The sun in front of us, fat and bold.
And you're in. Slicing through the surf.
I'm up to my knees and screaming.
'Rich! It's so fucking cold!'
But you swim away towards the sun.
Big mama sun in a red swim hat
sinks now, with no splash, under the waves.

THE SUNDIAL

Do not talk to me today because I want to be alone.
I am not sad or petulant; I just want to stretch out the space
between myself and where I sit on this lawn.

The cherry tree has bark like parchment
and my thoughts are the words written in an ancient script.
Don't forget to breathe. Don't forget to breathe.

Listen to the bee over the stonecrop flowers
and the blackbird's warning. I am not wanted here.
But I close my eyes and push my hands into the grass,

the summer grass not rained on for over two days now.
Today there is no sun and the wind has dropped.
There's not a single shadow on the sundial.

CLOUDS FROM AN AEROPLANE

What is this?
The snowfield between sleep and waking.
What colour is this?
Vanilla ice cream in lemonade soda.
What shape is this?
My grandmother's christening blanket.

What does it smell like?
My grandmother's christening blanket.
What does it feel like?
Vanilla ice cream in lemonade soda.
What noise does it make?
The snowfield between sleep and waking.

Where are you going?
Vanilla ice cream in lemonade soda.
When will you get there?
The snowfield between sleep and waking.
What place is this?
My grandmother's christening blanket.

AT ST ISSUI'S SHRINE

'I give thee most humble and hearty thanks
for all thy goodness and loving kindness to me.
Especially for this… and this… and this.'

On a clear day I think there would be a view,
but the chapel was wrapped in cloud like a special treat.
Three weeks past Whitsun and my breath was steam.
The walk up was tough. But not too tough, I thought.

St Issui was a hermit. His statue had a kind face.
There were fresh sweet peas and a sprig of birch in a vase.
I was breathing hard, so I knelt on the mat.
I was touched that someone took such care of this church.

Before the steep hill up I rested at the well.
There were little offerings hidden in the stones.
Bracelets, earrings, shells, ribbons.
On the tree nearby were more ribbons and a padded heart.

When I was much younger, men stopped in the street and turned.
But at the shrine I felt the power of age.
Slipped foundations create a charming slant
but lichen speckles gold on walls,
and that tiny well, older than the church,
is still the place where people believe in hope.

This… and this… and this.

WHAT IS LOVE?

What is love? I think it is a rainstorm.
Two people ran across the park to shelter under the tree.
He saw her at the gallery. She was wearing a flowery dress.
Now they can't stop talking. They are standing in a puddle.
They laugh and shake out their wet hair.
Marriages start like this.

What is love? I think it is a new house.
Piling up fast with stuff in every room.
How can she have so many dresses, shoes, cooking pots?
How can he have so many retro computer games?
One day they'll get a bigger house
but the stuff just keeps growing.
Children's clothes, teddy bears, floppy rabbits, shoes,
bicycles, more computer things, broken dolls, surfboards.
Suitcases, books, rucksacks and cake tins.
If a room is empty it doesn't feel like home.

What is love? I think it is the sunlight
on a July morning at a breakfast table.
They are both old now with icing sugar hair.
A hand held. Shh. Listen to the blackbird.
What's the song? Do they remember the beech tree and the
    rainstorm?
What's the song? It doesn't matter, but they never felt alone.

HOLIDAY COTTAGE SUNDAY

Once a woman scrubbed this stone floor on her knees
and a man hauled a sack of coal up the path.
I pretend to understand a rural life
by considering how the crocosmia
flames orange against the grey stone wall
and lavender smudges blue along the grass.

I have bought a week of quiet.
My career does not make my hands go rough.
I am pleased by uncomplicated tasks
like hand-washed smalls and scrambled eggs.
The dawn chorus woke me up at five.
I do not worry if the ewes will abort.

Remote means four miles from a shop,
but I did a Waitrose skim before I arrived.
I have cable television and Wi-Fi if I'm bored.
A shelf of John Grisham and Jilly Cooper books.
And a large-scale map to show me which way to walk
through waist-high dock and thistles to an unlocked church.

SHELTERING FROM THE RAIN
IN A COUNTRY CHURCH

after Larkin

I run across the graveyard much too fast
and push open the weighty door.
It shuts behind me with a clunk and the noise
of rustling anorak and wind in my ears calms down.
Replaced with whitewashed stone and carved wood.
The smell of damp granite, wet floors and mould.

I am not religious. My footsteps plonk
up the nave and I look around.
Victorian glass. Barrel roof. Unrestored. I know about churches.
One family holiday it rained for two weeks non-stop
and for entertainment we went to nearly every church in Suffolk.
Tiny Hopton. Grand Garboldisham. Forgotten Harling. Empty
    Blythburgh,
where, my father told us in a solemn voice, Cromwell's men
shot at the painted angels to bring them down.

I was twelve and uninterested. I wanted to be on my own
and read Narnia books, not admire clerestory windows.
This church has a rood screen. Thanks to Dad I know what a
    rood screen is.
It's fifteenth century, says the leaflet, a marvel. Pale oak. Carved
    with leaves.
Untouched by Cromwell's men because they didn't find this
    church
lost on a hill at the end of high-banked lanes.

Sweet peas by the altar. Tapestry kneel rests. This church is used.
A box of books. *Cope with Crisis. One Hundred Puddings.*
    Donations, please.
I read through selected psalms by David, in the Order for
    Evensong.
Why art thou so full of heaviness, O my soul: and why art thou
    so disquieted within me?

The rain has stopped. I like the feel of empty quiet. I have too often chosen this instead of company. I wonder how much I have missed.

I go outside and goldfinches skim across a wildflower meadow of blue campanulas and purple knapweed.

DRIVE THROUGH THE NIGHT

Don't be afraid to drive through the night
and go somewhere you have never been.
You won't know what you'll find until you get there.

When we were children you were never brave.
You didn't want to climb the apple tree
or steal plums from our neighbour's garden.
You collected stamps and cacti and old books.

But sometimes in the night, you said,
when you couldn't sleep, you crept downstairs
and sat on the old chair in the best room,
with the chaise-longue by the window and the grim carved
      sideboard.
You watched the shadows slide and merge.
You weren't scared, you said,
just wanted to make sure there was nothing scary.

Now you can be as bold,
going through an unfamiliar night,
to somewhere you have never been
and you don't know what you'll find until you get there.

Will you find a mountaintop with a silver palace?
An orchard of pink blossom and a unicorn?
A warehouse of rare and dusty books? I think you'd like that.
Or our front room back in Brickwall Lane
with you, not scared, but wide wide awake,
watching the shadows in case they move.

Or when you get there, there might be nothing.
Don't be afraid of nothing. Nothing isn't treatments, or
      operations,
or slidey shifty shadows. Nothing could be peaceful.

Don't be afraid on this long last night,
even if when you get there you find nothing.

AUBADE

When I woke up in the morning I thought you were there
and I turned over to find you weren't.
It was odd to have a cold space at the other side of the bed.
It took me a few moments to locate myself.
I was still half asleep and involved in a dream
about going to Hay-on-Wye to buy shoes
which was actually a memory of
a pair of shoes I bought on impulse and then
didn't wear them because they were too exquisite.
With pink leather flowers and wedge rope soles.
Espadrilles. You can't wear them in a British summer.

This wasn't home. This was somewhere else.
My bed was old-fashioned iron with a white eiderdown.
A conifer outside the cottage window shook its
branches like a wet dog. And made a noise
like whoosh. Some small bird – marsh tit? willow tit? –
chipped chipped. It was raining, but not hard.

At home, by now, the families would be
loading up their Škodas and Passats to take their offspring
to the better schools. The slam of car doors
and 'Where's my rugby kit?' The grunt replies
of dads late for jobs as architects, or mums,
barristers, council managers, sound up and down my street.

And you, with an enormous yawn, and a stretch of all your limbs,
would tell me, despite being sixty-one, how fit and energetic
      you still are,
and today you will go swimming or for a cycle ride.
And it's my turn to make a cup of tea.

But here the tree shook, and the bird chipped,
and the rain fell, like a mist.

HIGH SUMMER

High summer is regal.
Queen of the country tracks,
she's in her kingdom counting the heads of willowherb,
and St John's wort in graveyards.
The skeletons of hogweed.

A bus shelter covered in ivy
by a crossroads where the road dips
to a brown sludge of stream.
The sticky smell of meadowsweet.
Honeysuckle hair and eyes like brown moths.

Full bosomed and bellied, heavy and slow,
a pregnant Herefordshire cow,
brick-red wall in the sunburnt grass.
Doesn't move but flicks away flies.
She dreams of next year's king
growing fat inside her.

THE LAST DAYS

Go to sleep, little boy.
Tonight there will be no gas attacks or bombs.
We will hide in the basement and I will sing to you
about the flowers in my mother's garden.
Do you remember we used to play there

in the grass with your sister?
Do you remember how tall the grass used to be?
Do you remember your sister?
She used to say you were not brave enough.
Go to sleep, little boy.

I think I will try to sleep too. Before you were born
you were so small. You were like a little fish
and you slept safe in my sea cave.
I wish we could go back in time
and you would be safe and I could hold your sister.

Your father would pat my belly and be proud of us.
Perhaps I could go back further still
and sleep in my mother's sea cave
where all I can hear is her heart
and not the scream of these fighter jets.

Go to sleep, little boy. Do not grow up
and learn to hate.

THE PERSEIDS

I will leave my bed and go and find a hill
where I can watch the Perseids.
Lie in the grass
with the glow worms. The smell of hay and vetch
on the wind from the dry brook. Not cold.
The scratch of the stalks and the catch of my breath.
The sky dull after a day of hot.
This August night has faint stars.
Then they fall. One. Two. A slide of light. A scrap, a streak.
Then I see them all,
gold of the universe burnt in air.

Make a wish. Make a hundred.
I will leave my bed and walk away from here.
Walk right back to when I was twenty-three.
My baby wrapped in an old shirt.
His wisp of hair.
The smell of hay and vetch.
And I was young enough to
make a wish on the falling dust.

MY MOTHER'S GARDEN

Summer's over and the gales blow in from the west.
Bend the hollyhocks and chuck plums on the lawn.
Apples are falling but not sweet enough to eat;
their white taste makes my eyes water.

I have woken up to the clouds being punched
and a day when I am holding my breath
waiting for more bad news.
But the storm has passed and there is only debris.
A Tesco bag. A dustbin lid. A skid mark on a road.
A red shoe in a ditch.

The last flowers on the climbing rose are brown.
My mother's hands with skin like tea-stained silk.
She folds up newspapers in boxes.
Memories are being stored.

SHOP

I am a shop.
Because people walk in and say,
have you got any
lunch, Mum?
Clean socks?
Food. Always food.

I am a very small shop.
I am running out of stock.
I am up the highest shelves
and at the back of drawers.
Have you got any
patience, understanding?
Sandwiches, roast potatoes?
Cure for nightmares? Warm jumpers?

I am a disorganised shop.
I am often closed.
Especially on Sundays.
In the mornings I am full of sun
but by the afternoon
dark and gloomy.
People walk past and bang on my door.

Have you got any love?
Go away. I'm shut.

STILL THERE

I have a memory of you in Peterchurch.
We are in the car, parked near the gate.
I'm impatient. I want to go right now
and see the church, because I love churches,
and what's inside? Memorials? An ancient font? A brass?

You are absorbed in the map to work out
the best way back. I open the car door
and say, 'Come on!' and you say, 'No. Wait.'
In the avenue, leaves fall through sunlight.
Dry grass. Wet leaves. In Golden Valley.

It's afternoon and we are coming back from Hay.
Leaves and sunlight. The first smells of autumn.
Dry grass. Wet leaves and a hint of bonfire.
But we have never been to Hay or Peterchurch,
so this must have been with someone else,

but I can't think who. There is no man I know
who would sit there so calm and stubborn.
Perhaps it wasn't Peterchurch
and I have confused two memories.
A church and leaves. A man with a map.

When I remember this I can't seem to change it.
We are still there, in Peterchurch, Golden Valley.
I say, 'Come on!' and you say, 'No. Wait.'

KANDAHAR

I have been to Syria, Iran and Afghanistan.
But I am not a terrorist.
I was a student in 1978,
before the fall of the Shah, before the Taliban.

The one road from Herat to Kandahar.
A few lorries, a few scruffy cars
and our bright-painted Volkswagen Kombi van.
Three Cambridge medical students, and me,
in the back, taking it in.
I didn't think dry places could be so luminous.

Do not camp in the wild, our guidebook said.
Dress appropriately. Cover up.
I was not covered up. A vest, khaki shorts.
I was hot and dirty, not washed for days,
my hair a mess. My fingernails black.
We were singing 'Show Me the Way to Go Home'.

Then, there he was. Walking through the dust.
One man, with a turban. Tall. He flagged us down.
'Kandahar,' he said, and pointed up the road.
He sat opposite me. 'Kandahar,' he said again.
He had a rifle over his shoulder. Two strings of bullets round
    his neck.

He had green stone eyes.
A long beard. He put his hand on his Kalashnikov.
It was nearly four hours to Kandahar.
He was quite calm. Not like us.

Two miles outside of town.
We stopped.
He left. Walked off across the scrub,
his rifle high across his back.

Nothing there but rocks and sand.

INSTRUCTIONS TO THE CHURCH

At Stanton follow signs to Forest Coalpit
and take the road to Grwyne Fawr.
Yes, you can drive there, but I recommend you walk.
There's an interesting alluvial forest nature reserve
at Coed y Cerrig. (Valley of the stones.)

Linger there awhile and take in this opportunity
to experience the forest wetland flora from the broadwalk.
     (Very special.)
Follow signs to Patrishow, past the five-way crossroads.
It is approximately one and a quarter miles.
A steepish walk, so take plenty of liquids.

The road descends into a gully. I will come to that later.
Keep going up until you see the church porch on your right.
You will probably want a rest now. There is a handy bench
in the graveyard. It's a peaceful spot, so admire the view
down the valley and across to Twyn y Gaer.

The oldest part of the building is the shrine. Probably pre-
     Norman.
No, not Saxon. Welsh. The Saxons didn't come this far.
Note the crooked window, due to recent subsidence,
and the statue of St Issui in aluminium by Frank Roper. 1995.
This room was once a schoolroom. Then a store.

The church itself is twelfth century. The font is older.
You will, of course, notice the magnificent rood screen.
The loft is particularly rich, seventeenth-century openwork
     panels
on a horizontal beam of bressumer with running ornaments.
Notice the vine trail between two wyverns.

Of note also is the doom figure on the west wall
holding an hourglass, scythe and spade.
Notice too the biblical texts in red ochre.
The monuments are also interesting, mostly of
wealthy farming families in this region.

When you walk back, linger by the well.
St Issui was a hermit here, so the story goes,
until his murder by an ungrateful traveller.
(No written evidence.) Do not add to the junk deposited.
I come here every month and clean it up. It amazes me
that people still are superstitious.

MR PRICE'S GHOST

I was one of nine. Three died.
Two girls and a boy, all babies.
That happened back then, and I was the last.
My mam loved me the best. I was spoiled, see.

No hard work until I was ten. Dad was a carpenter.
Made furniture lasted fifty years and coffins.
Plenty of them. I helped him polish the sides
but I wanted books. The Rev. Phillips said, 'He's a smart one.'

Did well, I did. Walked two miles to Dorstone
for the Hereford train. Worked in accounts at Bulmers
for forty-five years. Dad died in '52, so I stayed with Mam.
Looked after her well. Meat every day. White cloth on the
table.

Mam died and I kept the place on. Just as nice.
Never married, I did. Wanted to once but Mam didn't like her.
Phyllis. Met a farmer in Bacton. Muck on the carpet. Mam was
    right.
Retired in '91. Grew potatoes and cabbages. Turnips and beans.

My raspberries were famous. And the sweetest gooseberries.
Never missed Hereford. Never missed the people.
Went to London once with my sister Helen.
Didn't like it. Never went again.

REMEMBER

You will not remember this.
You were fifteen months old and just walking.
A month after my father died.
It was the park in South Harting,
the one behind the council houses.
There were tall trees, I remember. Ash trees,
and there was a lake
and two ducks. Female. Drab.
It was a shady park, not much used.
One broken swing. Leaves on the lake.
I liked that lake.
You crawled across the grass
and then stood up.
Lifted your hands to catch the leaves.
Yellow and orange. You laughed and laughed!
Such funny leaves! Look at them fall!
You, in your yellow jumper. Orange trews.

OCTOBER HEATWAVE

Walk off the road and onto the track
down the ash-lined lane
where the puddles have all dried up
and the shade feels exotic
in this sticky heat. Through the gate

and the path follows the base of the Gaer.
Now, back in the sun, each step
brings a new patch of damp on your shirt
and a horsefly bites your shin.
At the top. Stop. Breathe. Look back down.

A glacier made that valley. You can see its sweep
on the road towards Llanbedr. Ice.
You would love ice right now on your neck
and on the swelling bite. The trees below are turning rusty.
There is one patch of shade
on an oak tree's roots where a lame sheep pants.

THE SMELL OF MIST

I have no shape and I am sort of transparent
like mist and sometimes
I am not there. Sometimes I think I can
smell myself, sort of acrid, like low mist
on an autumn morning. There is something
clingy about me. I stick to clothes and hair,
and I want to wash myself away,
wash myself away, or chuck myself
into the dirty clothes basket.
I am not a nice thing or a good thing.
I am trying to find beauty in myself,
see myself sort of hanging in the air
over the river, around the alder trees,
rather than a smell
on a dirty shirt to be chucked away.

CAN'T SLEEP

I can't sleep and the dark is treacle.
Stuck to the chest of drawers, the floor.
No point closing the curtains. It's black out there too.
And quiet. Quiet as the inside of a kitchen cupboard.
Quiet as the inside of a treacle tin.
Quiet as the inside of a treacle tin inside a kitchen cupboard.
Treacle. That's a funny word. Treak. Hell. Tweak. Well.
The treacle well of this room. Sinkhole to the end of a cave.
Things with no eyes live in caves. Don't think about them.
No mouths. Don't think about them. Or spiders. Did one just
      crawl
across my face? Gooey black inside a treacle tin. Doesn't
even taste nice. Sticky and burnt. Did I turn the cooker off?
Would I smell smoke before it choked me?
A charred body after a firestorm, arms raised like they are
      pleading.
Don't think about it. Or spiders.
Think about something like dancing.
In a field of buttercups. That field I walked through
this afternoon. All scattered sunlight on buttercups and
      feathered grass. Ticks.
Live in long grass. Bury in your skin and suck your blood.
I might have a tick. My leg is itching. Can you die from Lyme
      disease?
I should Google it. No. Turn over. Think about nice things.
An iced cake in a cake tin in a cupboard where there are no
      spiders.

HIPSTER CENTRAL

Whatever happened to the greasy spoon?
This cafe now does skinny lattes and eggs Benedict for brunch.

Sophie and Matt love it here. Sophie and Matt, both thirty-four,
left London and careers in a hedge fund
to buy original Edwardian features and a sense of place.
He's now a sustainable development consultant.
She makes jewellery out of vintage glass
which she sells on Etsy. She's branching into wood.

Their home was sound but needed 'colour'.
They sourced stuff from Freecycle
and reclaimed the floor. The antiques add a quirky touch.
They love it here. Especially now baby Io's arrived.
They can get organic cavolo nero in Open Ground.
Another shop sells Spanish cheese.

I have to say I love it too.
With my skinny latte and my new hipster shoes
I am reading, in German, Rilke's *Book of Hours*.

THE CARRIAGE WORKS

It was empty when I moved here
and it's still an empty hulk.
The Carriage Works up Stokes Croft.
Big. Bleak. Bland building once a factory.
A slab of neglect by the hipster bars.
A wall for street art, colourful and raw,
and graffiti, blurred,
and faded posters from long-gone gigs:
Brizzle DJ. Storm FC.
Cum. The Goggle crew. Bent and Co.

Behind the bricks buddleia grows tall,
and sycamores strain to reach the light.
Split bin bags and mattresses
burst out their guts. Discarded bits of bikes.
Tarpaulin where the homeless sleep.
Used needles shine in the nettle beds.

In the café the skinny guy in a furry hat
flips through his playlist on his new Mac Air
and the pixie hippy girl, all crinkled hair and floppy skirt,
Skypes her Swedish boyfriend in his Lisbon pad.
The street drinkers gather on a scrape of mud.

TIME AND THE RIVER

Your mind moves on smooth lines. Your thoughts, not like mine,
put memories in databases. Each one marked and kept in the
    computer room
in the storehouse. Down the corridors, long corridors
bend with purpose. Events, you tell me, are not linear
but weave like a basket folded in on itself. Holding all moments.
We exist at all points. Spread out in space.

My mind is a basket. A junk shop fish basket. Holding bits of
    old spools,
two broken watches, twelve handkerchiefs, pink lipstick,
    damaged twine.
Each day there's something I had forgotten but then remember.
Like that day we walked the path by the Severn, mud up to our
    ankles.
I can smell the water now. Fishy like old seaweed, seeped out
    of the mist,
and you telling me there is no river of Time.

A POSTCARD FROM MY FUTURE SELF

It gets worse. I have to tell you this,
but you learn to live with it.
We all learn to live with it
and those who don't have a bad time.

Like, really bad. But some things stay good.
I know who my real friends are.
The ones who are still alive, anyway.
I can buy chocolate even though it's hard to find.

Don't go to Paris. It's not a good idea.
You will fall down the steps
in Montmartre and take two months to recover
and miss that other holiday in Prague

where he was going to propose. I found out later.
Don't buy that shiny blue dress. It makes you look fat.
I found out later. Don't vote Labour. Because of the war
which you don't know about yet.

NUMBERS

My father went to buy bread, but he did not come back.
For two days he did not come back.
My mother cried, so did my sisters.
My uncle said, 'You must leave for Europe.
Find us a new home and we will follow.'

One was a doctor from Damascus.
His wife and children were already in Toronto.
Two were cousins, fourteen and fifteen.
They smoked and laughed but their eyes were scared.
Three were chemistry students from Aleppo.
Like me they were the hope for their families.

In Izmir we slept on the streets and waited for the smugglers.
One thousand, two hundred euros to cross a barrier of water.
Six were from Afghanistan.
A man, his wife and four children.
I sang to his little girl. Her name was Noor.

Seven were a whole family from Hama.
They used to run the town's best restaurant.
One said, 'Your father was a good man.'
I cried then because I knew he was gone.

The boat was not big enough. We all knew this.
In the dark in the ocean it took in water.
I can still hear the children cry. I can hear the grandmother pray.
When we saw the lights on the land the young men swam.
'Phone the coastguard!' I shouted to Noor's father.
'Phone the coastguard and they will rescue you!'

Ahmed, the doctor, made it to Toronto.
He sends me messages of hope on Facebook.
I'm in the mud in Calais with Yousef, Abdo, Touma.
'One day,' we say, 'we will find a home. One day we will be
    married.'
I think about my sisters and Noor's shy smile.
In the UK, I hear, they now spit at strangers.

GLITTER (WITH JANE GLENNIE)

Mama, please cover me in glitter.
I want glitter on my nails and glitter in my hair and glitter on my
    face
and glitter everywhere.

I want to sparkle like the treetop girl.
The girl with wings and a magic wand and a gold shimmy dress.
I want to be like her.

I want to sparkle so my friends in my class
will want me to sing at their pamper parties.
I want to sing like Ariana Grande sings 'One Last Time' on the
    roof
with a purple sky and the fireworks.
I want to be like Elsa in *Frozen*,
throw off my glove and make snowsteps in the sky.
Let it go, let it go, let it go.

No, my daughter.
Be the glitter from within.
Be the sparkle you already are.
Make the magic through your own work and creation.
No need to be like Elsa. Be who you are.

If you wake up tomorrow and you can make snow
we'll learn to rebuild the icecaps,
we'll make a polar bear den,
we'll preserve food for the hungry.
No one needs glitter.

THINGS I FOUND IN THE HEDGE

A spider's web pearled with dew.
Hawthorn blossom. A pair of pink underpants.
A flock of sparrows. Always loud.
A thrush's nest with four sea-blue eggs.
Walkers Cheese and Onion crisp packets. Two.

A white sports sock with a worn red trim.
A white butterfly on a nettle bloom.
A dead fledgling wren. I tucked it in the leaves.
Meadowsweet and the smell of a fox by the drain.
A green beetle with an iridescent sheen.

A used tampon. Who would put it there?
Hawthorn berries. Crimson. Gritty. Hard.
A string of bryony. Purple, orange, green.
A bus ticket. A Coke can crushed.
A Lidl bag. A clump of ginger hair.

A Kit Kat wrapper and a dropped Mars bar
turned white after a night of frost.
The skeletons of hogweed. Brittle twigs.
An ankle-deep puddle with an oil rainbow.
The blackthorn blossom just begun to flower.

SOLSTICE

Hush.
Even in the dark days
there is hope.

Think beyond the light failing
on this grubby afternoon
when all the room turns to shadow
and the grey shapes rise
in the corners of your eye.

Hush.
Turn in your bed now.
Turn again and let your life fade.
Beyond this night
in the dark garden the snowdrops
have already found
their white petals.

The lace of your wedding dress
you are ready to wear once again.

ACKNOWLEDGEMENTS

I would like to thank my PhD supervisors, Dr Kate Pullinger and Dr Bambo Soyinka, for their advice and support during the creation of this project.

The poem 'A Manual Of Wonder' was created from an account of recovery written by David Richardson.

I would also like to thank my filmmakers who have created the film versions of these poems. Many of the films have been screened at short film and poetry film festivals. It has been a most wonderful and creative journey. The filmmakers are: Helena Astbury, Marie Craven, Cheryl Gross, Cinema Fragile, Cactus Chilly, Jack Cochran, Helen Dewbery, Kathryn Darnell, Lori Ersolmaz, Claire Ewbank, Pamela Falkenberg, Jane Glennie, Janet Lees, Matt Mullins, James Norton, Marc Neys, Maciej Piatek, Marcia Pelletiere, Jutta Pryor, Carolyn Richardson, Stevie Ronnie, Lucia Sellers, Othniel Smith, Sarah Tremlett, Eduardo Yague.

For further details of all the collaborators for The Book of Hours please see the website at http://thebookofhours.org

9 781911 570370